THUNDERSTICK

THUNDERSTICK

Kenneth T. Williams

Thunderstick
first published 2010 by
Scirocco Drama
An imprint of J. Gordon Shillingford Publishing Inc.

Scirocco Drama Editor: Glenda MacFarlane
Cover design by Terry Gallagher/Doowah Design Inc.
Author photo by Stefen Winchester
Printed and bound in Canada on 100% post-consumer recycled paper.

We acknowledge the financial support of the Manitoba Arts Council and The Canada Council for the Arts for our publishing program.

Library and Archives Canada Cataloguing in Publication

Williams, Kenneth T., 1965-
Thunderstick / Kenneth T. Williams.

A play.
ISBN 978-1-897289-52-5

I. Title.

PS8645.I4525T48 2010 C812'.6 C2010-905868-2

J. Gordon Shillingford Publishing
P.O. Box 86, RPO Corydon Avenue, Winnipeg, MB Canada R3M 3S3

For Lorne Cardinal, who never stopped believing.

Characters

Jacob Thunderchild is a Cree journalist in his mid to late 30s. He's in bad physical shape and beginning to suffer some of the effects of his alcohol abuse. He works for the *Ottawa Citizen* covering Parliament Hill.

Isaac Thunderchild is Jacob's cousin. He's about the same age but he's taken much better care of himself, physically anyway. He's a photojournalist who's covered some of the worst wars in the 90s.

Setting

Ottawa and Northern Ontario, 2000.

Acknowledgements

There are many people and organizations responsible for making Thunderstick the success it is today. I'd like to acknowledge the support of Native Earth Performing Arts, Kennetch Charlette and Donna Heimbecker from Saskatchewan Native Theatre Company, Layne Coleman from Theatre Passe Muraille, Del Surjik from Persephone Theatre and Bradley Moss from Theatre Network. I'd also like to thank Lorne Cardinal, Paul Thompson, Tim Hill, Ryan McMahon, Curtis Peeteetuce, Mark Dieter, Ian Ferguson, Craig Lauzon and Cheryl Millikin. And finally, a special thank you to my agent Charles Northcote.

Production History

Thunderstick premiered at the Saskatchewan Native Theatre Company, Saskatoon, in November, 2001, with the following cast:

JACOB..Mark Dieter

ISSAC .... Curtis Peeteetuce

Directed by Lorne Cardinal

Set Design by Kennetch Charlette

Lighting Design by Tim Cardinal

Costume Design by Jeannette Munroe

Set Design / Stage Manager Scott McDougall-Ryan

A subsequent production was mounted by Theatre Passe Muraille, in Toronto, in April, 2002. It was directed by Paul Thompson and starred Ian Ferguson and as Jacob and Tim Hill as Isaac. Ian injured himself during the run and had to be replaced by Lorne Cardinal.

Persephone Theatre and Theatre Network co-produced it for the 2009 / 2010 season. It was co-directed by Del Surjik and Bradley Moss, and starred Lorne Cardinal and Craig Lauzon who both played Isaac and Jacob, alternating roles each performance. It was presented in Saskatoon on the Persephone mainstage in October, 2009, then again in Edmonton at Theatre Network in January, 2010.

Kenneth T. Williams

Kenneth T. Williams is an award-winning Cree playwright and journalist from the George Gordon First Nation. His plays *Thunderstick, Suicide Notes, AWOL: Aboriginals Without Official Leave* and *Three Little Birds* have been professionally produced across Canada.

He recently co-wrote an adaptation of *Are We There Yet,* a play for young audiences about sexual decision-making. He's just finished another play for young audiences, *Baby Daddy,* about teenaged Aboriginal fathers and is currently working on another TYA play, *My Bestest Friend Ever*. The sequel to *Thunderstick, Bannock Republic,* recently had a successful run at Saskatoon's Persephone Theatre.

Act I

Scene One

JACOB's apartment. Signs of a bender. JACOB is in rough, rough shape, face down on the floor. Slowly he gains awareness of his situation. As he speaks, he tries to find the bathroom.

JACOB: I…I…I am a paramecium. Crawling around the floor. Blindly groping… Need to puke. Hope I find the toilet first. Hope. At least I have that. Most paramecia don't. Speaking hurts. I am still speaking even though it really fucking hurts. Why does it hurt? Why do I say paramecia and not parameciums? Why am I asking myself these stupid questions? Must record this. Remind myself why I should not drink.

Searches himself for the mini-recorder he's hidden in his shirt. His coordination is shot.

New symptom. Hands have turned to flippers.

He manages to hit record. He crawls to the bathroom.

I can't… I can't… I can't live like this anymore. No motor control. My brain is crawling out of my eyes. Moving hurts. OK God! I promise! I will not drink again. Ever. If you don't believe me, just kill me! Please, kill me. A bolt of lightning. A stray bullet. A meteor the size of Texas. Anything. End the misery.

His head bumps the toilet.

It's a simple request God. Kill. Don't taunt.

JACOB sticks his head in the bowl and flushes. ISAAC enters.

ISAAC: Jacob?

JACOB: Wow. The spray feels refreshing. That's not a good sign.

JACOB pukes then flushes. ISSAC walks towards the bathroom. JACOB's head is still in the bowl.

ISAAC: Jacob!

JACOB: God?

ISAAC: No. It's Isaac!

JACOB: Isaac. Isaac who?

ISAAC: Isaac Thunderchild!

JACOB: Cousin Isaac!

ISAAC: Look, the door was open and— Oh Jesus!

JACOB barfs again.

JACOB: What are you doing here? Thought you were in Africa or some place?

ISAAC: I'm back in Canada now.

JACOB: Cool. Welcome baaaaaaak—

JACOB hurls again.

ISAAC: How drunk are you?

JACOB: Just a little. But it's for a good reason.

JACOB gropes for the recorder then shows it to ISAAC.

I'm recording it.

ISAAC: Why?

JACOB: For when I'm sober and the need to booze it up hits me.

He pulls his head out of the bowl and stands. They move to the living room.

Cousin! You've gotten older…and blurrier.

ISAAC: You're not making sense. You need to remember this?

JACOB: Speak into the mic. That's a good reason. But I won't remember if I don't record it.

ISAAC: *(Into the mic.)* You act stupid when you're drunk.

JACOB: OK, OK…I don't think that's what you said earlier.

ISAAC: Jesus. Some things never change.

JACOB: Tell me about it. It's been fifteen years and you're still an uptight, preachy bastard.

ISAAC: I'm not here to preach. I'm here because I was told to pick you up for an assignment.

JACOB: You and me?

ISAAC: Yep.

JACOB: You're working for the *Ottawa Citizen* now?

ISAAC: Started today.

JACOB: That calls for a celebration.

Goes for a bottle of booze.

ISAAC: No, man, we got an assignment!

JACOB: Man, you must've pissed somebody off if they sent you to me.

ISAAC: They teamed me up with you when they heard I was your cousin.

JACOB: You told them that?

ISAAC: No. They thought we were brothers.

JACOB: We look that much alike, eh?

ISAAC: Yeah, I can't tell you how proud I am.

JACOB: Speak into the mic. I need to remember why I didn't miss you. What's the assignment?

ISAAC: Forget it. I'm not going to the Hill with you in that condition.

JACOB: The Hill? What happened? Someone threw a pie at the man again?

ISAAC: Not this time. Apparently one of his ministers is missing.

JACOB: Who's missing?

ISAAC: Justice, I think.

JACOB: Elaine Hawley? You saying Elaine Hawley's missing?

ISAAC: Yeah. Missing.

JACOB: What do you mean "missing?"

ISAAC: Missing! Gone. Vanished. Disappeared. I guess there's a budget vote today and she's not around.

JACOB: The budget vote. Shit, that's bad.

ISAAC: Apparently. Look. We've got to be on the Hill in half an hour to scrum the "da Boss" before the cabinet meeting.

JACOB: Half an hour? Cabinet doesn't meet until ten. What is it now? Midnight?

ISAAC: It's nine in the morning.

JACOB: Right. Right. OK. I'll be right with you. Just let me freshen up.

ISAAC: How about you sleep this bender off and I'll tell 'em you have a doctor's appointment.

JACOB: No! They'll send that dip-shit Hal to cover this.

ISAAC: Is he sober? Or are all you guys at the Citizen raging drunks?

JACOB: He's sober. He's always fucking sober. That brown-nosing puke almost got me fired last month. He said my demeanour offended his Mormon val-yoooooooze.

He pukes again.

ISAAC: Yeah, they're right bastards, eh? All that focus on faith, clean living and hard work.

JACOB: Hey, I'm sensitive about other people's belief systems.

If I knew he was a graduate of Brigham-Young, I wouldn't of poured that rum into his diet-caffeine free coke.

ISAAC: You spiked his drink!

JACOB: It was diet and caffeine free! What the hell is wrong with these people? No booze. No coffee. You wonder how they make it through the day.

ISAAC: OK, OK, whatever. Look, you are not ready for this.

JACOB: I am so ready for this. Relax. You think this is the

first time I've shown up drunk? I'm a professional. I know how to handle falling off the wagon.

ISAAC: I think you crashed and burned the wagon this time.

JACOB: You calling me a wagon burner?

ISAAC: Get your ass in gear! This is no time for joking!

JACOB: Geeeze. Lighten up, princess.

JACOB manages to stay on his feet while he rifles through his medicine cabinet. He pulls out Alka-Seltzer tabs, bottles of Pepto, Rolaids, and Tylenol, plus, surprisingly, a bottle of Hai Karate cologne.

ISAAC: They still make Hai Karate?

JACOB: That's for later.

JACOB quickly mixes the Seltzer and Tylenol, then slugs it back, followed by a bottle of Pepto, and a fistful of Rolaids.

Give me a minute. I'll be as good as new.

ISAAC: I think I'm going to be ill.

JACOB belches.

JACOB: See. A new man. Now for the chaser.

He sprays himself liberally with the Hai Karate, then into his mouth like a breath spray. ISAAC pulls the bottle away.

ISAAC: Whoa whoa whoa!

JACOB: For the mouth bunnies. Better than mouthwash. It's go time!

JACOB drops like a stone. ISAAC tries to pick him up.

ISAAC: This is not a good idea. You're going to get fired if you show up like this.

JACOB: I'm fine I'm fine I'm fine. Honest. I'm fine. I'll probably get fired if I don't go.

ISAAC: Really? You call this fine? You need help.

JACOB: I need to do this. I need to keep my job. I can't lose that as well. Not today. Not today, man. Not today.

ISAAC: What happened?

JACOB: Her name's Jenny. She left me a note.

JACOB fishes a crumpled note out of his pockets and hands it to ISAAC.

ISAAC: "Dear Loser."

JACOB: It says "lover" not "loser!"

ISAAC: No Jake. l-o-S-e-r.

JACOB: You sure that's not a V?

ISAAC: It's an "s."

JACOB: She called me a loser?

ISAAC: Actually, she called you a "stupid loser."

JACOB snaps the note away from ISAAC and stares at it blearily.

JACOB: Where?

ISAAC: Right there.

JACOB: I thought that said "stud."

ISAAC: Come on stud. The Prime Minister is waiting for us.

Black out.

Scene Two

ISAAC and JACOB are in a jail cell. Jacob is leaning against the bars, ISAAC is lying on the bunk.

ISAAC: I can't believe you puked on Chretien!

JACOB: This is outrageous! They can't hold us this long.

ISAAC: Jacob, you barfed on the leader of this country. They can hold us here until we rot.

JACOB: If any of my notes are missing, there's going to be hell to pay.

ISAAC: Your notes! What about our jobs!

JACOB: We're political prisoners and all you're worried about is a paycheque.

ISAAC: This is not about politics. This is Canada. Wherever I was in this world, Canada was a beacon of human rights. I was always told how lucky I was to be from Canada. You know why? Because Canada just doesn't arrest its citizens for no reason.

JACOB is about to say something.

Shut up, I'm not done. There's a good reason we're here, Jake. We're here because you projectile-vomited all over Chretien. We're in here because some foul smelling, pink shit spewed from your mouth onto the PM's chest and half of the parliamentary press gallery. We, not just you, but we are in here because just as the RCMP are hauling you away, you start screaming, "Isaac! Isaac! Save me, cousin!" And then you start puking on them. And then they think I'm part of your bizarre assassination-by-vomit plot!

Pause.

JACOB: So. You're saying this is my fault.

With surprising ferocity ISAAC grabs JACOB, shoves his head in the toilet and flushes it repeatedly.

ISAAC: Yes! I'm saying it's your fucking fault! It's entirely your fault! And every goddamned moment was caught on television!

ISAAC lets him go and collapses on the bunk.

JACOB: You know, you should see a therapist. You have an anger management problem.

ISAAC: That's some diagnosis coming from an A.A. refugee. What's your sponsor going to say when he sees you publicly drunk on national television? Doesn't that revoke your status as an "anonymous alcoholic?"

JACOB: I gave up on him a long time ago.

ISAAC: The booze is going to kill you, you know.

JACOB: This from a guy who dodges bullets to take pictures. I'm amazed you're still alive. Amazed and disappointed. Is it hot in here or is it just me?

ISAAC: It's just you.

JACOB: I need a drink.

ISAAC: You were just stone raging drunk a couple of hours ago.

JACOB: Well it's worn off, if you hadn't noticed. Let me the fuck out of here! You can't hold us this long! This is a violation of our rights! We're journalists! You can't arrest us! Christ! My head hurts.

ISAAC: It's assault. Of course they can arrest us. And not only that, but you've diverted all the attention away from Elaine Hawley.

JACOB: What do you mean?

ISAAC: With the show you gave? The lead news story won't be Minister Hawley's disappearance. If I wasn't there from the beginning, I'd think you were part of some cover up. A way to get people to forget about her.

Pause.

JACOB: What do you think really happened to Hawley?... Do you think she's been kidnapped?

ISAAC: Don't ask me. It's your town, Jake. Any other unusual happenings?

JACOB: Well... Bonnie Nass hasn't been seen in a while.

ISAAC: Who?

JACOB: Bonnie Nass. The National Chief. Come to think of it. She's kind of disappeared too.

ISAAC: Well case closed. They're probably hiding out together.

JACOB: You know, they could be.

ISAAC: What? These two hiding out together? I was just kidding.

JACOB: Look, Nass was elected chief just as Hawley became minister of Indian Affairs. And they got pretty cosy during that time.

ISAAC: Cosy? What the hell does that mean?

JACOB: All-night, closed-door meetings. Weekends together.

ISAAC: That's part of their jobs.

JACOB: Look, personally, what people do in their own bedrooms is their own business. But, and I'm saying it's not my own personal belief, even though I don't understand it totally, but I'm not condemning it, but there are people, more people than we'd like to acknowledge, but there are people who…frown upon that sort of thing.

ISAAC: And?

JACOB: They're always together. At the same conferences. At the same signing ceremonies. Holidaying together without their husbands.

ISAAC: Husbands? Right There goes your theory.

JACOB: No. They're not married anymore. In fact, they both got divorced right around the same time.

ISAAC: You're not trying to tell me divorce is evidence of lesbianism?

JACOB: Would explain my three ex-wives.

ISAAC: Why? Are they dating each other?

JACOB: No…No! Look, even after Hawley was promoted to Justice, they still managed to find ways to work together. This could be the story of the year, Isaac.

ISAAC: Right. "Justice Minister in lesbo love connection with National Chief." The *Citizen* will love that headline. And since when did a woman dumping her man mean she's gay?

JACOB: Maybe it does.

ISAAC: So, using your logic, Jenny is a lesbian. Is that right "stud lover?"

Pause. Ouch, that hurt.

ISAAC: I'm sorry. I'm sorry. I didn't mean to, you know, bring up Jenny… Really, I'm sorry.

JACOB: You don't understand, Isaac. I love her. I love her so much. I'd do anything to get her back.

ISAAC: Then check yourself into rehab and get sober.

JACOB: Except that.

ISAAC: It's fucking up your life but you won't quit?

JACOB: It helps me cope with the job, alright!

ISAAC: Maybe you should quit that too.

JACOB: Give up my career? Don't be ridiculous.

ISAAC: What career?

JACOB: I'm a dedicated journalist.

ISAAC: Who's more dedicated to drinking and self-destruction. You should be a senior editor by now instead of clinging desperately to some low-level reporter's gig. And Jenny…is this how you treat the "love of your life?"

JACOB: We had our anniversary last month. I packed a picnic and we went to Meech Lake in Gatineau Park. It's beautiful there.

ISAAC: I'm amazed.

JACOB: Then that goddamned Alliance MP, James "Big Jim" Roberts, got himself shot and the boss called me on the cell screaming at me to get to the hospital.

ISAAC: On your day off.

JACOB: I forgot to file the paperwork. Besides, parliament was supposed to be on a summer break! But no.

While all the other good Alliance guys were back having barbeques and square dances in Alberta, Big Jim got shot by "assailants unknown" and interrupts my anniversary picnic!

ISAAC: You're the one who fucked up. All you had to do was file some paperwork and the day was yours.

JACOB: I told her I'd make it up to her.

ISAAC: How? By drowning yourself in the Ottawa River?

JACOB: You're just as unreasonable as she is.

ISAAC: When you say things like that, I can see how she's a fool for leaving.

JACOB: You've made your point.

ISAAC: You've got to face responsibility, Jake. You're closing in on 40 and—

JACOB: I said, I don't want to talk about it anymore! You're givin' me a bigger headache with all this preaching.

ISAAC: I don't preach.

JACOB: You do so, you sanctimonious bastard. "You're irresponsible." "You're a bad journalist." "You turn women into lesbians."

ISAAC: I'm just reporting the facts.

JACOB: That my life sucks and it's my own fault? Old news, Ike. Find some new copy.

Pause.

This is a hot story.

ISAAC: It's not a story. It's a theory. A bad theory. There's nothing to support this.

JACOB: There you go again. Preaching.

ISAAC: Convince me that there's even one small, plausible lead to all this.

JACOB: Let's start with Chretien again. What did he say at the scrum?

ISAAC: Before or after you puked on him?

JACOB: Funny. Very funny.

ISAAC: Because what he said after was the most coherent thing he's ever said—in English or French.

JACOB: He's pretending everything's hunky-dory even though Hawley missed the budget vote.

ISAAC: Then you made everything "chunky" dory all over his chest.

JACOB: You just don't miss a budget vote unless you're dead. But he's going on about how everything is just fine.

ISAAC: Which leads us to a lesbian love nest?

JACOB: Yes!

ISAAC: I was just kidding!

JACOB: OK, OK. Forget the lesbian angle. And Nass. The minister has disappeared, and we're supposed to act like this is normal—like ministers go missing everyday. Somebody is hiding something.

ISAAC: What?

Pause.

JACOB: What if I told you I might know where Hawley is?

ISAAC: I'd say everyone else does too.

JACOB: No... I know...something...

Pause.

ISAAC: Are you going to make me guess?

JACOB: Can't tell you…they might be listening.

ISAAC: Well I've stopped listening. Have fun chasing this one.

JACOB: You're not going to help?

ISAAC: No. There's no story. And I don't want to get into any more trouble with you.

JACOB: You have to help.

ISAAC: Why?

JACOB: You're my cousin.

ISAAC: And?

JACOB: And… I'm going to need a great photographer.

ISAAC: The *Citizen* has other photographers.

JACOB: Nobody wants to work with me.

ISAAC: That's a sad statement if that's true.

JACOB: I'm a sad man, Isaac! You've already said so. This is my last chance. And I need your help, cousin!

Pause.

ISAAC: I'll think about it.

Black out.

Scene Three

JACOB's apartment. Lights up reveal…nothing.

JACOB and ISAAC enter.

ISAAC: Make it quick. You still have time to file a story. I never thought your drunken ramblings would do any good. But once they heard "hands have turned to flippers" on your tape…

They both stare at the empty space.

Are you sure this is your apartment?

JACOB runs offstage to the kitchen. ISAAC discovers a note in the middle of the floor and picks it up.

"Dear Stupid…"

JACOB returns.

JACOB: She left me with nothing! Her furniture, her computer, her towels, her TV, her stereo, her dishes, my booze, her phone, her fish tank. My booze. She took all her stuff back. And my booze!

ISAAC: She left a "Dear Stud" note.

He takes the note.

JACOB: "Dear Stupid." You know…"If you think there's even a remote chance for this relationship then meet me at seven tonight at Darcy Magee's." Oh God, not Darcy's.

ISAAC: Why Darcy's?

JACOB: My anniversary picnic.

ISAAC: Yeah?

JACOB: I told her to wait for me there and I'd meet up with her right after I filed the story.

ISAAC: So?

JACOB: I didn't. I guess she's still kind of sore.

ISAAC: Well, you better show up this time. And quickly. You barely have an hour to get cleaned up and get over there.

Pause.

You're not going, are you.

JACOB: My instincts are telling me that we're sitting on the story of our careers.

ISAAC: Is this story worth losing "the love of your life" over?

Pause.

JACOB: Could you meet her for me and let her know that I'd be there but—

ISAAC: No!

JACOB: Come on, Isaac—

ISAAC: No!

JACOB: I'd do it for you.

ISAAC: I wouldn't need you to. I'm not that insensitive or immature.

JACOB: I am not immature.

ISAAC: Are so.

JACOB: Am not.

ISAAC: Are so.

JACOB: Am not.

ISAAC: Oh Christ! You were like this as a kid. Stubborn, stubborn, stubborn. I'm not bailing you out of this. And you shouldn't be asking me to.

JACOB: I'm not asking, I'm begging. We're family!

ISAAC: You've already tried that on me and it still won't work. Being your cousin does not make me your slave. I am not working with you! I am not going to get in the middle of your sorry relationship. And even though we're working at the same paper, I don't want anything to do with you!

Pause.

JACOB: Is that supposed to hurt? Because it doesn't. I'm tougher than that.

ISAAC: It's a fact, not an insult.

Pause.

JACOB: I know this story is important. And I know no one else has the angle that we have. They couldn't think of it.

ISAAC: We made it up.

JACOB: It's a viable hunch.

ISAAC: It's an outright lie.

JACOB: But it might be true. Look…listen up, just listen up for a second… Hawley has a secret hideaway…up north…near Muskoka.

ISAAC: And how do you know this?

JACOB: Can't tell you right now.

ISAAC: And what? You want me to just ignore my survival instincts and just trust that you know what you're doing?

JACOB: Yes!

ISAAC: No! I need a break. I didn't come back to run around the woods of northern Ontario looking for wayward cabinet ministers. I need a rest. I just want to take pictures of politicians kissing babies. That's why I picked Ottawa.

JACOB: But that's all boring stuff.

ISAAC: Exactly. I want peace and quiet. You can only watch people murdering and maiming each other for so long…go to another country…same fucking thing…over and over again for 15 years…nothing changes…and then Zia…

JACOB: Who's Zia?

ISAAC: Forget it.

JACOB: "Maiming, killing, maiming, killing, then Zia." Then this "look." Who was she? Someone important?

ISAAC: Leave it alone.

JACOB: A girlfriend?

ISAAC: A colleague.

JACOB: Oh no, no, no, you don't get that look for just a colleague.

Pause.

Hey, look, Isaac I'm not going to let up until you tell me, so you might as well tell me. Who's Zia? Who's Zia-who's-Zia-who's-Zia-who's—

ISAAC: Zia Markaavi. She worked the CNN bureau in South Africa. We worked together a lot.

JACOB: Is she hot?

ISAAC: She's…dead.

JACOB: Sorry.

ISAAC: Cancer. It was advanced when the doctors discovered it. She died in six weeks. Just faded away in front of me. Peacefully too. Like she was just falling asleep. Fifteen years shooting war zones. Seen thousands get shot and blown up. Even some of my own colleagues. But after Zia died, I couldn't go back.

JACOB: Why not?

ISAAC: It was then I realized that no one really lives in a war zone. They're either dead or dying. But I believed my presence meant something. That my pictures would be seen around the world and people would care…they would do something…I at least cared enough to be there. I had hope that help would come. But then it all just stopped meaning anything to me.

JACOB: After Zia was gone?

ISAAC: Yeah.

JACOB: She sounds like she was more than just a friend.

ISAAC: She was. She was…my wife.

JACOB: You were married?

ISAAC: Two years ago.

JACOB: I can't believe this. I feel so betrayed.

ISAAC: Betrayed?

JACOB: You didn't invite me. You didn't even let me know!

ISAAC: It's not like you could've afforded the airfare to South Africa?

JACOB: Give me some credit. I would've sent you a gift. A card at least. I would've been happy for you. But you didn't even call me.

ISAAC: Alright. Fine I didn't call. I'm sorry.

JACOB: Bullshit. You are the worst liar, ever. I'm sorry your wife died, Ike. I really am. She must've been one hell of a woman. But now you tell me I've lost a cousin I didn't even know. It's like a chunk of me is missing. Jesus, I can't believe you did that. I always told you when I got married.

ISAAC: I thought it had lost its meaning since you'd done it so often.

JACOB: There's you and then there's me.

ISAAC: What the hell does that mean?

JACOB: We're different. That's all. Fuck. How can you even work? Take a real vacation. Get away. Grieve. Wallow in self-pity. You've earned it.

ISAAC: I'm not like that.

JACOB: Then get "like that." Are you becoming Super Ike? The man of steel? Trust me, it'll get lonely in that fortress. Stop building walls.

ISAAC: Is that more A.A. bullshit?

JACOB: At least I know to be honest about my emotions. You miss her Isaac and you can't even say it.

ISAAC: Don't tell me how I'm feeling!

JACOB: Well show some fucking emotion!

Pause.

I know why you can't take pictures anymore. These victims of war…they've become people… They are now human beings…not subjects at the other end of the lens. You finally know how they feel. Do yourself some good and get out of here.

ISAAC: What?

JACOB: Get lost. Go. Take off.

JACOB opens the door.

ISAAC: What the hell is your problem?

JACOB: You have the problem.

ISAAC: That's funny, coming from an alcoholic.

JACOB: At least I know I'm an alcoholic. You don't even know how to act human.

JACOB pushes ISAAC out the door and shuts it.

Christ. I need a drink.

Black out.

Scene Four

It's night. JACOB is seated on a park bench near the Rideau Canal, drinking from a paper bag. ISAAC walks up to him slowly.

ISAAC: Hey.

JACOB: Hey.

ISAAC: Can I sit down?

JACOB: I don't own the bench.

ISAAC sits.

ISAAC: How'd it go with Jenny?

JACOB: She saw the news. That pretty much sealed the deal.

ISAAC: She was mad?

JACOB: Not mad. Just, in her words, "so terribly disappointed in so, so many ways."

ISAAC: What you drinking?

JACOB: You gonna start preachin?

ISAAC: No. No, just wondering if I can join you?

JACOB: Sorry. It's only tonic water. Want some?

ISAAC: Ugh. No. Too much sugar. That stuff will rot your teeth.

JACOB: What are you doing here? I thought I told you to scram.

ISAAC: I just got back from the office. Look, I hate to tell you—

JACOB: I already know.

ISAAC: Who told you?

JACOB: Hal, bless his lily-white heart. He came by and told me they have a box of my stuff at security. I can pick it up any time. He just capped off a perfect day. And then he hugged me.

ISAAC: He hugged you?

JACOB: Yeah. He then told me that God loves me.

ISAAC: Really?

JACOB: Yep. "God loves you, Jacob." Then he gave me a book of Mormon.

ISAAC: Did you take it?

JACOB: Oh yeah. And just as he was almost out of the door at Darcy's, I wung it at his head. Nailed him right at the base of the skull. "God loves you too, Hal! He just has a fucking funny way of showing it!"

ISAAC: OK, that explains his crying jag when I saw him at the office.

JACOB: Oh great. I'll have to make amends for that later. Some things are just not worth getting sober for.

ISAAC: You're quitting drinking?

JACOB: I don't know. Hitting him in the head with that book felt soooooo good. How am I supposed to say sorry for that when I know the next time I see him I'll want to do it again.

ISAAC: I didn't know getting sober was so complicated.

JACOB: Well, thank you for the good news. Who are you teamed up with now?

ISAAC: No one. I quit.

JACOB: Really?

ISAAC: You were right. I need a vacation. A real vacation. I've just never had one before and I don't know where to start.

JACOB: A cruise is nice.

ISAAC: I don't know how to play shuffleboard.

JACOB: You'll get the hang of it. Jenny and I went on a cruise once.

ISAAC: Was it fun?

JACOB: Don't remember. I was seasick. I was too busy throwing up to notice. Jenny confined me to our room for the rest of trip.

ISAAC: You weren't throwing up overboard, were you? In front of the passengers?

JACOB: I wanted to work on my tan.

ISAAC: How much browner do you want to get?

JACOB: I had a new Speedo I wanted to show off.

ISAAC: Christ, and I thought I saw some awful shit in Africa.

JACOB: You laugh now. You should've seen me when I was working out. Buff.

ISAAC: So what happened?

JACOB: Buffet. More temptation than I could handle.

ISAAC: There are fitness programs, you know.

JACOB: And then there's A.A. There's all sorts of help for a loser like me. But there's no cure for a broken heart.

ISAAC: Oh please. Now you're getting maudlin.

JACOB: Is that a crack about my weight.

ISAAC: No. Maudlin. Overly insincere melancholy.

JACOB: Hey! There's nothing insincere about my melan-whatchamacallit. My girlfriend dumped me. I'm in pain, you know.

ISAAC: I thought you'd be used to it by now.

JACOB: Look. My three ex-wives? When they dumped me, I just took my stuff and left. No big deal.

ISAAC: No big deal? Lawyers, courts, dividing assets.

JACOB: Naaah. Splitting up assets was easy—I didn't have any. Of course my third wife thought I was secretly rich and hiding my money. I said, "What, and pretend to live like this?"

ISAAC: Why didn't you marry Jenny?

JACOB: She said no. That's when I knew she was the girl for me.

ISAAC: You've lived a weird life, Jake.

JACOB: Maybe I should write a book one day.

ISAAC: I don't know. Do you think you could find the time?

Pause.

JACOB: You been watching the news?

ISAAC: Hawley hasn't turned up yet and her family refuses to speak to anyone.

JACOB: Did you find out who's now covering it for the *Citizen*?

ISAAC: Your buddy, Hal.

JACOB: I'm sure numb-nuts will do them proud. I phoned the national chief's office today. Nass isn't there.

ISAAC: You didn't ask if she was bunking with Hawley did you?

JACOB: Do I look that stupid?

ISAAC wants to but doesn't say it.

I merely asked if she was on vacation.

ISAAC: And?

JACOB: "She's consulting with chiefs." That's code for "she's unavailable because we don't know where she is."

ISAAC: So what do you think?

JACOB: You already know what I think.

ISAAC: So what now?

JACOB: I'm thinking about it.

ISAAC: Where does someone get a drink around here?

JACOB: Darcy's is just around the corner.

ISAAC: Do they have a TV? Maybe we should keep an eye on the news.

JACOB: Yeah, they have a TV. That's how Jenny found out. Christ. They just kept showing me puking on Chretien over and over again. A couple of times in slow motion. I have to admit, that look on his face was priceless when he realized what was about to hit him.

JACOB & ISAAC: *(Imitating Jean Chretien.)* Taaaberrrnaaaaac!

JACOB: Jenny just kept shaking her head like she'd been

expecting this moment for a long, long time. Everyone in the place was laughing.

ISAAC: Considering your past record, I thought she would've forgiven this episode.

JACOB: She did. Doesn't mean she wants to stay with me anymore though.

ISAAC: Was it an ultimatum?

JACOB: No. She's not like that. She was just tired of me tripping myself up.

Pause.

ISAAC: You have a car?

JACOB: What?

ISAAC: A car. I hear Muskoka is pretty this time of year.

JACOB: No.

ISAAC: No, you don't have a car?

JACOB: No, you're not going with me.

ISAAC: Why not? You were practically begging me in jail.

JACOB: That was before…

ISAAC: What? Zia?

JACOB: Yeah.

ISAAC: She told me to keep on working.

JACOB: Uh huh. And probably something about how it would be okay to see other women, even get remarried?

ISAAC: Yes.

JACOB: And…you really believe that?

With that ferocity we saw in the jail, ISAAC grips JACOB by the throat and pulls back his fist to hit him.

ISAAC: FUCK YOU!

Pause.

JACOB: Go ahead…hit me…pound me into the dirt.

Slowly, ISAAC regains his control and lets go of JACOB.

ISAAC: You didn't know her!

JACOB: I know women. I understand them.

ISAAC: Where does this expertise come from, asshole? Your string of healthy relationships?

JACOB: Three ex-wives and one ex-love-of-my-life-girlfriend. Impeccable credentials, believe me, when it comes to understanding women.

ISAAC: Bullshit.

JACOB: You were really in love, weren't you.

ISAAC: Of course.

JACOB: So in love, you'd sacrifice anything for each other.

ISAAC: Is there a point to this?

JACOB: She was dying. She knew she was dying. Do you think she wanted you to suffer as well?

ISAAC: I was suffering.

JACOB: But you weren't the one dying. You were going to live. She knew that better than you did. She was already missing you—probably breaking her heart she was never going to see you again—and probably very afraid to die, she still needed to let you know that it would be alright to go on living without her. That it would be okay to find happiness again.

Pause.

ISAAC: You're full of shit.

JACOB: You would've done the same thing.

ISAAC: But I would want her to find happiness again.

JACOB: Exactly! Are you looking for "happiness" now?

ISAAC: No.

JACOB: Are you going to get over her?

ISAAC: I hope not.

JACOB: Right. How do you think Zia would feel if she knew that then?

ISAAC: I won't find another woman. Not one like her. I won't. So what's the point?

JACOB: The point is Zia didn't want you to die with her.

ISAAC: I wish I did.

JACOB: Oh, Jesus Christ, Ike! Who's "maudlin" now? For a guy who's seen all the death and cruelty you have, you sure have a romantic notion of the world. Or is that what made you go to the war zones in the first place? Some sort of death wish thing?

ISAAC: You didn't know her!

JACOB: You don't know yourself.

ISAAC: What the fuck does that mean!

JACOB: You said it yourself. Wars are full of the dead and dying. I was wrong earlier. They're not people to you. They are you. You're practically dead. That's you you see at the other end of that lens. And you're very fucking afraid to look at yourself.

Pause.

JACOB: You know. It's okay to lose control once-

ISAAC: I don't lose control.

JACOB: Oh right. Putting up the walls. I forgot.

ISAAC: I have seen a starving mother—only skin and bones—try to nurse her dying baby. I've had friends mutilated by landmines. And I have seen a boy, with a burning tire around his neck, scream for death. And you know what I have to do when I see that Jake? I have to take their picture. I have to put the camera up to my eye, make sure it's in focus, make sure the exposure is right, and take their picture so the rest of the fucking world will do something about this fucking ugliness. I cannot be emotional to do that job. And, yeah, maybe, I take too many risks which would make it seem like it's some stupid death wish thing. But at least I got off my ass and tried to do something about it. For fifteen fucking years I tried to do something about it! Can you understand that?

JACOB: I think so.

ISAAC: Good. I'm going to Muskoka with you.

JACOB: It still doesn't feel right. You should be away, on vacation.

ISAAC: That will be a vacation for me. At least I won't have to worry about dodging bullets.

JACOB: Don't be so sure. It's hunting season.

Black out.

End of Act I.

Act II

Scene One

Lights up reveal a beat up Reliant-K. ISAAC is under the engine tinkering with it and JACOB is reading a map.

Pause.

ISAAC crawls out from underneath.

ISAAC: I should've taken the cruise.

JACOB: OK okay, I think I know where we are.

ISAAC: You think? You didn't know that Muskoka wasn't north of Ottawa!

JACOB: So I got turned around a little! I've got it situated!

ISAAC: Does it matter? That piece-of-shit car of yours isn't going anywhere. I don't know what's wrong with it, but a priest and a bucket of holy water wouldn't hurt.

JACOB: Hey! Don't insult my Stella. She's been my constant companion for 10 years.

ISAAC: Of all the women in your life, it's your car that you're devoted to?

JACOB: I can tell you without a word of a lie that she was a hell of a lot more comforting than any of my three exes.

ISAAC: It's not a woman! It's a car! A Reliant-K car.

JACOB: Maybe it's just a car to you, mister. Maybe you see her as just transportation. But I spent many lonely nights in her when I'd been thrown out. She never chucked me out. If I ever needed a place to go, she was always ready and willing. So stop calling down my car.

To Stella, soothing.

It's OK baby, the bad man's gone now.

ISAAC: OK. It's your twisted life. I'm just a passenger.

JACOB: A preachy passenger.

ISAAC: Get rid of the map.

JACOB: We're almost there.

ISAAC: We're not going to get there in that thing! We got other things to worry about. It's getting dark, and it's getting colder. I'm freezing. It feels like winter.

JACOB: It's not that bad. It's actually kind of nice for October.

ISAAC: I'm not used to it anymore

JACOB: Well you'll appreciate Stella more when you have to stay in her tonight.

ISAAC: I don't know if I'm comfortable with that. I'd feel like I'm sleeping with one of your ex-wives or something.

JACOB: Yeah, well, sleeping with one of my ex-wives would serve you right for talking about Stella like that. You know, we're not far from Hawley's cottage.

ISAAC: How far is not far?

JACOB: About 2 inches.

ISAAC looks at the map.

ISAAC: Two inches? That's 20 miles. You plan on walking that?

JACOB: You know, I'm in pretty good shape.

ISAAC pokes him in the belly.

ISAAC: No wonder you don't feel the cold.

JACOB: That's it, you're sleeping in the bush tonight.

A wolf howl in the distance.

ISAAC: What was that?

JACOB: A wolf, I think.

ISAAC: Are there still wolves in Ontario?

Another howl.

JACOB: Sounds like it.

ISAAC: Maybe they're just coyotes.

JACOB: Either way, I'm sleeping in the car.

ISAAC: So am I.

JACOB runs for the door. ISAAC cuts him off. They wrestle for the door. JACOB, using his larger size, wins and hops into the car and locks all the doors.

Let me in Jake!

JACOB: Not until you apologize.

ISAAC: Apologize!

JACOB: Take back what you said about my car.

ISAAC: OK, I'm sorry I made fun of your car.

JACOB: You didn't mean it.

ISAAC: I did too.

JACOB: We already went through this. I know when you're lying. And you're not apologizing to me.

ISAAC: You're kidding.

JACOB: It's that or you're sleeping with the wolves.

ISAAC: I am not going to apologize to your car!

JACOB: You hurt Stella's feelings.

ISAAC: Are you out of your fucking mind?

JACOB: You're not getting in with an attitude like that mister.

ISAAC: Don't be stupid!

JACOB: Let me explain "stupid" to you, stupid. "Stupid" is not apologizing to a car and being eaten by wolves.

ISAAC: I will not degrade myself like that!

JACOB: There's no one here except you, me and Stella. Who's going to see you get on your knees, kiss the hood ornament, and beg forgiveness from a car?

ISAAC: Get on my knees?

JACOB: Did I forget to mention that?

ISAAC: Let me in right now!

JACOB: OK, just kiss the hood ornament.

ISAAC: On a K-Car!

Wolves howl. Closer now.

JACOB: I think they're getting close. You'd better make up your mind fast.

ISAAC thinks about it. He's almost on his knees.

JACOB: She likes a little tongue.

That's it. ISAAC pulls out a cell phone and starts dialing.

What are you doing? Calling wolf?

ISAAC: I'm phoning some of your friends and letting them in on our little adventure.

JACOB: What?

ISAAC: Yeah. I'm going to ask for Hal at the *Citizen* and give him a little tip.

JACOB: You wouldn't.

ISAAC: I won't if you let me in—Hello! Yes…News please… Yes, I'll hold.

JACOB: Don't lie. I know when you're lying!

ISAAC: Am I lying now?

Pause.

News? Yes. Is Hal in? Yeah, Hal. The nervous guy who blinks a lot. Can you check?

JACOB runs out of the car and grabs the cell phone.

JACOB: Man. You don't play fair.

Wolves howl. Much closer. ISAAC and JACOB both run for the car and after some scuffling, they both get in and close the doors. Then they both smell something awful and use the doors to fan out the car.

Sorry. It happens when I get nervous.

They close and lock the doors.

JACOB: What would our ancestors think of us? Hiding in a car because of some wolves.

ISAAC: That it was a reasonable thing to do.

JACOB: I thought we were supposed to have a spirit connection with wolves or something.

ISAAC: How would I know? I went to residential school. You're the one who got to hear all those stories from your old man. Weren't you listening?

JACOB: I just remember him winging beer bottles at me. That kind of interfered with our teacher-student relationship.

ISAAC: I remember you and him going out to the bush all the time.

JACOB: More like I was dragged out. Fuck I hated those trips. "Gonna teach you to be a real Cree, boy. Toughen you up." All that meant was me doing all the fucking work. Cutting wood, carrying all his shit and dodging beer bottles when he threw them at me.

ISAAC: Beer bottles?

JACOB: Fuck ya! Beer bottles. Wine bottles. Rye. Whatever he had handy. He'd wing it at me and yell, "duck!" Sometimes he'd just throw the bottles without any warning. Just because he was drunk, didn't mean his aim was bad. Jesus, he could hit anything he aimed for. Drunk or sober. That's why I knew he never aimed for my head. Bottles would explode around me and I'd jump. Other times, he'd just yell, "duck!" And I'd duck. Then he'd laugh because he hadn't thrown anything.

Pause.

Shit, when I heard that the band would pay for my education, I went back to high school, did everything I could to get my grades up. Got into that Indian college in Regina.

ISAAC: At least he was proud of that?

JACOB: No.

ISAAC: No?

JACOB: Fuck no. He didn't want me to go to school. "It's a white man's world, shithead! What makes you think you're going to amount to any-fucking-thing out there!" And then I'd say, "Yeah, well Isaac's going to university…

ISAAC: What?

Pause.

JACOB: Nothing.

ISAAC: Well, what did he say to that?

JACOB: He'd just scowl and smile. You know, that really evil smile he had.

He imitates the smile. Pause.

Were you scared?

ISAAC: Of what?

JACOB: Going to university in another country?

ISAAC: No. I was more scared of being stuck on the reserve. When was the last time you went back?

JACOB: Not since my old man's funeral. I had to make sure the bastard was really dead.

ISAAC: That was over ten years ago.

JACOB: Yeah well…nothing much has changed…just more kids. How come you never went back?

ISAAC: No reason to.

JACOB: You know Dr. Thompson spoke about you a lot. He was really proud of you. Proud like a father.

ISAAC: How did you know him? You went to the school in town.

JACOB: I needed some help with my English to get into college. I asked him to tutor me. Every time I went there he'd go on about how you were going to his old university. How he'd pulled some strings for you and stuff to get into Oxford. He said he even wrote you some letters.

ISAAC gets out of the car.

ISAAC: I don't think those wolves are coming anymore.

JACOB gets out of the car.

JACOB: What?

ISAAC: Nothing.

JACOB: Is it something I said?

ISAAC: Good call, Jake. Or was that just a lucky guess?

JACOB: Jesus, you don't have to be so fucking sarcastic.

ISAAC: If you're so fucking bright then figure it out.

JACOB: You don't have to explain anything. I heard the stories. But he never tried anything to me.

ISAAC: Alright. Great. You got away.

JACOB: He didn't…with you, I mean—

ISAAC: I don't want to talk about it! Fuck! Take a hint!

JACOB: Sorry.

ISAAC: We've got other things to worry about…Like how are we going to stay warm.

JACOB: Easy. We just build a fire.

ISAAC: I don't think a fire's a good idea. If we're anywhere near this secret hideaway—as you say we are—then a fire would attract attention. Which is something I've been meaning to ask.

JACOB: What?

ISAAC: How do you know about this place if it's such a major secret?

JACOB: Ex-wife number two. If I tell you more than that, she'll track you down and kill you in your sleep.

ISAAC: Uh-huh. And you've seen this place?

JACOB: No one gets to "see" the place, Ike. It's a secret.

ISAAC: But you've been up here before?

Pause.

Jake, tell me you've been up here before.

JACOB: I would…but that would be lying.

ISAAC: You mean we're lost.

JACOB points to the map.

JACOB: I know exactly where we are! We're right here!

ISAAC takes the map and spins it around.

ISAAC: North is that way, white man!

JACOB: Still doesn't mean we're lost!

ISAAC finds a big stick and picks it up.

ISAAC: Yes. This'll do.

JACOB: I thought you didn't want to build a fire.

ISAAC: Oh no, I'm not going to build a fire with it, Jake. I'm going to beat the everliving shit out of you with it.

JACOB: Ike! Calm down, Ike!

ISAAC chases JACOB around the car.

ISAAC: I am calm, Jake. I am in complete control. I am doing this as a rational human being.

JACOB: Wait wait wait wait wait! I got something that'll keep us warm. In the trunk.

ISAAC stops chasing JACOB. JACOB opens the trunk and pulls out a 40oz of rum.

Ta da! This'll keep your motor running.

ISAAC: Alcohol. Perfect. At least our corpses will be preserved.

JACOB: Do you have to be such a sourpuss all the time?

ISAAC: I'm being realistic.

JACOB: Well it's depressing.

JACOB opens the bottle and takes a long slug.

Whoa momma! That hits the spot.

ISAAC: Give me some of that.

JACOB hands him the bottle.

JACOB: Careful.

ISAAC: Yeah-yeah.

ISAAC takes a quick pull and chokes.

Fuck!

JACOB: Pretty good, eh?

ISAAC: I can't breathe!

JACOB: Easy. Easy. Just relax.

ISAAC: I think I'm gonna die.

JACOB: Don't panic. Just relax. Everything's normal.

ISAAC: Normal? I'm on fucking fire and I can't breath!

JACOB pounds ISAAC on the back.

JACOB: Is that better?

ISAAC: NO!

JACOB pounds harder, ISAAC struggles to stand up.

Stop it, you son of a bitch! Are you trying to kill me!

JACOB: Well, you're a surly drunk.

ISAAC: I think I'm gonna puke.

JACOB: That's it. You're cut off.

ISAAC: What is that!

JACOB: Overproof rum. 1-5-1. More bang for your buck.

ISAAC: You learn that in A.A.?

JACOB: This put me to A.A.

ISAAC: Jesus. I feel dizzy.

JACOB: Just relax. Breathe. Breathe. You'll be alright.

ISAAC: No. Got to stay focused. Or else we won't get out of here alive.

JACOB: Look. We stick out the night in the car. Stay warm with some liquid sunshine here. And we call for help in the morning. You don't have to be such a crybaby about it.

ISAAC: Call for help with what?

JACOB: Your phone.

ISAAC: It doesn't work. We're in a no-service area.

JACOB: But you just phoned the *Citizen*.

ISAAC: No, I didn't.

JACOB: I saw you.

ISAAC: I lied.

JACOB: Don't pull that on me. I know when you're lying.

ISAAC: Am I lying now?

Pause. JACOB looks into ISAAC's eyes.

JACOB: Yep. You're right. We are fucked.

ISAAC: Now what are we going to do?

JACOB: Bottoms up.

JACOB takes another shot of rum.

ISAAC: Is that your answer to everything?

JACOB: Works for me.

ISAAC: We need to be clear headed right now.

JACOB: No. I don't know what you need to be. But I need to be drunk.

ISAAC: What? And just wait for the world to roll all over you?

JACOB: Better to be limp when it hits. Less pain that way.

ISAAC: No wonder you've had such a stellar career.

JACOB: You're beginning to sound just like my old man. Here's the bottle. You wanna pop me with it?

JACOB holds the bottle to ISAAC, who doesn't take it.

You know what's funny? He was a drunk. An asshole. He stole from me. But right now he could walk into those trees with just a knife and some matches, make himself a fire and comfortable place to sleep. The bush was his home. He wouldn't have to wait for help.

Pause.

ISAAC: Jake, about your dad—

JACOB: I wonder if my life would've been better if I'd gone to the res school. I don't know what's worse? Getting drilled in the back with beer bottles by your old man? Or getting felt up by some boney English bugger? At least I could've sued the church.

Pause.

ISAAC: Do you remember the time Thompson was in the car accident?

JACOB: Yeah, vaguely.

ISAAC: It wasn't…an accident.

Pause.

One day, after supper…we'd just finished evening chapel and Thompson had taken some of the boys fishing on the other side of the lake, across from the school…we'd done our chores early all week and this was our reward…well, we didn't catch anything and it was getting late and we started back for the school…I don't know how it happened but the other boys were way ahead and it was just Thompson and I trailing…he was talking to me about how good my grades were and shit like that…

JACOB: Look, you don't have to tell me this.

ISAAC: Just let me finish. Alright. I need to finish this.

JACOB: OK.

ISAAC: Thompson and I are pretty much alone. It's getting dark. And he…he puts his arm around my shoulder…just rests it there…and he keeps talking about how I could go to university…and he slows down…so the other boys are way ahead now…and he's telling me how smart I am…how I'm not like the others…

Pause.

And that's when I saw your dad.

JACOB: My dad.

ISAAC: He was just in front of us…just off the trail a bit… in the bush…he's staring at us…and he's crying… really hard.

JACOB: My dad? Crying?

ISAAC: I mean. He's not weeping and wailing, but the tears have drenched his face…even in the dark, I can see the redness in his eyes…Thompson doesn't see him…I stop walking…the way your dad looks frightens me…something's wrong…Thompson turns to me…he looks at me funny…I think he wonders why I've stopped…and that's when your dad attacks him.

JACOB: He what?

ISAAC: Just with his bare hands…I watch your dad just beat the shit out of Thompson…and he's crying while he's doing it…sobbing…like I've never seen a man cry before…Thompson is knocked out…unconscious on the ground…but your dad just keeps hammering him…I finally get my wits together and I try to run to the school but your dad grabs me...and I almost shit myself because I think I'm in for the same...but he hugs me... tightly...and he's still sobbing...his whole body is just shivering... "you've got to be tough, boy," he keeps saying...over and over... "you've got to be tough, you've got to be tough"...he then let me go.

Pause. JACOB takes a long pull on the bottle.

Look. I'm not asking you to just forgive your father—

JACOB: Just what the hell are you asking me to do? He's gone. Can't bring him back. Don't want him back. He had a fucking shitty life. So did a lot of people. What are you going to do?

Drinks again, more this time.

ISAAC: Drink you fucking face off? That's productive.

JACOB: "That's productive!"

ISAAC: This is no time to feel sorry for yourself.

JACOB: After that fucking story! No, feeling sorry for myself is exactly what I plan to do! You can join me if you want.

ISAAC: It's no excuse to get drunk.

JACOB: If you hadn't already noticed, that's how I handle stress. Try it. You might like it.

ISAAC: Do you like it?

JACOB: Oh I love it! I can't get enough of it!

ISAAC: Give me the bottle.

JACOB: Fuck you!

ISAAC: Give me the fucking the bottle!

JACOB: Come and get it!

ISAAC: I'm not going to fight you for it.

JACOB: Why not! 'Cause my dad ain't here to protect you? Huh! That it! 'Cause I pounded the shit outta him once before! I can fucking do it again!

Pause.

Fucker had it coming. Oh man, did he ever have it coming. It was just one bottle too many. It was the last time I was home. Just got back from college after my first year. Got a summer job at the *Regina Leader-Post*. Wanted to share that with him.

Pause.

Motherfucker tells me to shut the fuck up. I tell him "you shut the fuck up!" He's pumping back some rye. A big forty. And he nails me with it. Right in the jaw.

He swings the bottle.

Thoomp. Stupid bastard. Forgot that they didn't make out 'em out of glass anymore. It was just a big plastic jug. He starts to laugh. But he's got that evil look in his eye. He woulda laughed if it was glass or plastic. And that's when I start hitting him…I never went back…except for the funeral.

Pause.

ISAAC: Give me another shot. I'm cooling off.

Black out.

Scene Two

Lights up. The stage is the same as before. ISAAC, wearing a sleeping mask, is cocooned in a sleeping bag. JACOB is nowhere to be seen. Noises from the Serengeti. An elephant trumpets. ISAAC moans and begins to wake up.

ISAAC: Ohhhhhhkay God. I'll never drink again.

ISAAC struggles to free himself of the sleeping bag but can't.

Oh Christ!

He rolls around, still locked in the sleeping bag, desperately trying to free himself.

FUCK! HELP! HELP! FUCK! HELP!

ISAAC scrambles out of the sleeping bag as if it were the jaws of a crocodile. Pause. He suddenly feels the incredible pain in his head and falls to his knees.

FAWWWWK!

JACOB enters carrying a full rum bottle, sandwiches and a thermos.

JACOB: Jesus, look who's barking in the weeds. But it's a good thing you're up.

ISAAC: Where the fuck am I and who the fuck are you?

JACOB: Where are your cameras?

ISAAC: My cameras? In the trunk.

JACOB opens the trunk and starts pulling them out.

ISAAC: Wait wait wait. Who are you again?

JACOB: I'm your driver. How do you work these?

ISAAC: Don't fucking touch those!

JACOB: We gotta go! Come on, let's go!

ISAAC: Just hang on a second!

JACOB: What?

ISAAC: Jacob… What are you doing in Africa?

JACOB: We're not in Africa! Look…Elaine Hawley… hideout…lesbians…Mounties…drink this…we gotta go!

JACOB offers the bottle to ISAAC.

ISAAC: You sick bastard! That's what nearly killed me!

JACOB: It's only water. Here.

ISAAC sniffs the bottle.

ISAAC: This must be some horrible nightmare.

ISAAC gulps down some water.

JACOB: Hey, hey, hey there cuz! That's all we got. Come on!

JACOB runs for the exit, ISAAC crawls back into the car.

ISAAC: I'm in a lot of pain.

JACOB pulls ISAAC out.

JACOB: No no no no no! I need you take some pictures for me!

ISAAC: Of what?

JACOB: Open your eyes, Ike.

ISAAC: Can't… Hurts.

JACOB: Ike! I found her! I was looking for water and I almost walked right into Hawley's compound.

ISAAC: Minister Hawley?

JACOB: Do I have to spell it out for you?

ISAAC: Yes. I can't think this morning.

JACOB: Don't have time. Here. Coffee. Sandwiches. I'll explain on the way. It's go time!

JACOB exits with camera gear. Pause.

ISAAC: Lesbian Mounties?

JACOB re-enters grabs ISAAC and drags him off.

Black out.

Scene Three

A clearing. ISAAC and JACOB enter, trying to be quiet. JACOB trips.

ISAAC: Shh!

JACOB: Why do you have so much gear?

ISAAC: You want the shot? You need the gear.

ISAAC pulls out a camera body from his bag, then a huge, honking lens—600 mm for those who want to be accurate—from the bag JACOB is carrying.

JACOB: No wonder that was so heavy.

ISAAC: Shhhhh. Man, you're loud.

ISAAC connects the body to the lens. He aims it at the cabin.

JACOB: See anything?

ISAAC: Two Mounties.

JACOB: Female?

ISAAC: Hard to tell under all that kevlar.

JACOB: Can I look?

ISAAC: There's a pair of binoculars in the bag.

JACOB pulls out the binoculars and looks towards the cabin.

There's someone else.

JACOB: Where?

ISAAC: Wait. She's walking around the living room.

JACOB: Is it Bonnie Nass?

ISAAC: Don't think so. This is a white woman. What the hell is she doing here?

JACOB: Who?

ISAAC: Amber LeClerc.

JACOB: Amber LeClerc? That's Amber Roberts. Big Jim's wife.

ISAAC: Big Jim?

JACOB: That Alliance MP who wrecked my anniversary.

ISAAC: I swear that's Amber LeClerc.

ISAAC pops out the spent roll of film from the camera and reloads it.

JACOB: Who's Amber LeClerc? 'Cause she's a dead ringer for Amber Roberts.

ISAAC: A friend of Nelson Mandela's. She was part of a big scandal in South Africa. Years ago. People thought the police murdered her.

JACOB: I never heard of it.

ISAAC: Don't you ever watch the news?

JACOB: Jenny cancelled the cable. Said it was making me fat.

ISAAC: Who's the guy with the cane?

JACOB: Holy shit! That's Big Jim. I thought he was dead.

ISAAC: We are definitely onto something here.

JACOB: But no Bonnie Nass.

ISAAC: Sorry cuz. This ain't no lesbian love nest.

JACOB: So what the hell…why would Hawley be hiding the Roberts?

ISAAC: Don't ask me…wait!

JACOB: What?

ISAAC: Someone else is in the cottage. Just entered the living room.

JACOB: That's her! That's Bonnie Nass! I knew it I knew it I knew it!

ISAAC: Shhhhhhhh.

JACOB: I was right Isaac. I was fucking right. They are lesbians. I told ya, I told ya.

ISAAC: Are you fucking stupid! That's not the story here.

JACOB: Then why are they lip-locked on the front por—

A gun shot in the distance. JACOB hits the dirt. ISAAC keeps taking photos.

What the fuck!

ISAAC: Shut up! Stay down.

Automatic rifle fire from all directions now. ISAAC turns towards where the fire is coming from.

JACOB: What are you doing!

More gunfire, shouts from all directions. ISAAC keeps taking pictures. JACOB cowers behind him.

Let's get out of here!

JACOB tries to drag ISAAC away.

ISAAC: I got to know something Jake. Where did you get that sleeping bag?

Bullets are flying everywhere. ISAAC, in his element, calmly reloads the camera.

JACOB: You're gonna get us killed!

ISAAC: And the coffee? Sandwiches?

JACOB: You're fucking nuts. Let's get out of here!

ISAAC: Let me know then I'll go.

JACOB: Found a hunting camp. No one was around. Took what I needed.

The shooting stops. Police shouts O.S. "Drop your weapons! Keep your hands up!" Etc.

ISAAC: OK. I don't think they were hunters. Take a look.

JACOB: Is it safe?

ISAAC: It's never safe.

JACOB peers up with the binoculars.

JACOB: Where did all those cops come from?

ISAAC: Don't know. But let's get out of here. Now.

ISAAC's phone rings—"Oh Canada", ring tone. They freeze.

Fuck!

Dogs bark in the distance. Phone rings again. ISAAC searches himself frantically, trying to find the phone. A helicopter approaches.

JACOB: What do we do?

ISAAC: Run, you idiot!

They exit running. The phone keeps ringing. Dogs barking increases. Helicopter louder.

Black out.

Scene Four

Lights up reveal ISAAC and JACOB in a holding cell.

ISAAC: This is familiar.

JACOB: I thought you said your phone was in a no-service area.

ISAAC: It was.

JACOB: Why didn't you turn the damn thing off?

ISAAC: Jacob, calm down.

JACOB: You also said there weren't any lesbians!

ISAAC: Will you get off the lesbians. That's not the story here.

JACOB: But I was right about Nass and Hawley.

ISAAC: You're missing the point, Jacob. You're not a gossip columnist. You're a journalist.

JACOB: No one's going to believe us without the pictures.

ISAAC: They will believe you because you are a witness. Write what you saw—a firefight in Ontario between a group of Afrikaaner terrorists and the RCMP—a refugee from apartheid hiding out in Canada—the Liberal minister of justice protecting an Alliance MP. It's too crazy not to be true.

JACOB: And I've got the minister of justice kissing the National Chief!

ISAAC: You've got a one-track mind.

JACOB: But I was right about—

ISAAC: Yes, you were right. I admit it.

Pause.

JACOB: You did get the picture, right. Of Nass and Hawley kissing.

ISAAC: Yes, I got the picture. I got it all…I just hope I can get to the film after we get out of here.

JACOB: If we didn't have to carry all that camera gear, we would've got away.

ISAAC: We? You mean you. You ditched all my stuff and crashed through the bush faster than a rhino on steroids. I just managed to hide the film near the creek before the dogs got me.

JACOB: You notice those dogs…they were all female.

ISAAC: Oh Jesus…

Pause.

JACOB: What do you think is going to happen?

ISAAC: Simple. They'll interrogate us, check out our story, and once they're sure we're just a couple of journalists who got lucky, a cavity search—boom—we're out of here.

Pause.

JACOB: Indians never catch a break.

Black out.

Scene Five

JACOB's apartment, a week later. JACOB is seated in a worn down easy chair, holding an unopened bottle of champagne. Otherwise, the place is empty. ISAAC knocks, then enters.

JACOB: It's open!

ISAAC: Hey cuz!

JACOB: Ike. Jesus. I thought you were Jenny.

ISAAC: Really? We look that much alike?

JACOB: No, I meant I was expecting her because she's lending me some furniture until I get back on my feet and heard someone and thought it was her—why are you here?

ISAAC: I'm taking off.

JACOB: No.

ISAAC: Yep. You were right, I need a vacation. So I'm going on a real holiday.

JACOB: How can you do this to me? Not now. Not when I need you the most.

ISAAC: Look Jake, I have to—

JACOB: Help me! Christ, how can you be so selfish? Especially now. I just got a promotion.

ISAAC: I heard. Congrats.

JACOB: Congrats? I'm very vulnerable right now and it's

your damn fault! If you hadn't given me all that great background info on South Africa my article wouldn't have any sense. None. And your photos sealed the deal.

ISAAC: You got a promotion because you wrote a great article. You broke the biggest story of the year, possibly the decade.

JACOB: And the editors are going to expect more great articles, cousin! Do you realize the expectations they have? They're like spoiled children. It's gimme gimme gimme all the fucking time! Then there's the tantrums. I'm not good around kids, Ike. They scare me. *(Hyperventilates.)* Christ, I need a drink.

Pops the champagne and slugs and chokes.

ISAAC: Easy easy easy…relax.

JACOB: *(Choking.)* I forgot. It's got no booze in it.

ISSAC takes the bottle, sniffs it and recoils.

ISAAC: And it's Canadian. You must really hate yourself.

JACOB: What am I going to do, Ike? I can't handle this pressure…sober.

ISAAC: Calm down.

Plops him into the chair.

JACOB: I am calm goddamnit! Look at me! *(Grabs ISSAC by the collar.)* It's not even my first day back and I'm a nervous wreck!

They struggle, ISAAC pushes JACOB off, who falls ass over tea kettle in the chair. JACOB turtles on the ground with the chair on top of him.

Issac, Isaac! Save me cousin!

ISAAC: Oh geez.

ISAAC helps him up, dusts him off.

Listen to me, Jake, and listen good. I need to go. I have to travel this country. I've been away for far too long and I've forgotten a bunch of things that I need to relearn. Rekindle a fire that I didn't know went out.

JACOB: A journey of self-discovery.

ISAAC: Something like that, yeah.

JACOB: Can I come with? Stella's got a new tranny.

ISAAC: No.

JACOB: She runs great, except for that shimmy and the brakes are a little spongy but she'll get us—

ISAAC: No!

JACOB: Why not!

ISAAC: How can I discover anything about myself if I'm always worried about a boozed-up retard!

JACOB: I quit drinking, you know.

ISAAC: I know. I'm happy for you. Stick with it.

JACOB: We make a great team. Jacob and Isaac, crusading Indian jounalists.

ISAAC: Good luck, cousin.

JACOB: Come on.

ISAAC: I promise not to be such a stranger.

JACOB: I missed you, cousin. I really did. Fifteen years is a long time.

ISAAC: I missed you too.

JACOB opens his arms, inviting ISAAC to hug him. ISAAC eventually relents.

JACOB: Just one thing's been bugging me, cuz.

ISAAC: What's that?

JACOB puts ISAAC into a headlock.

JACOB: Where's you hid the film? Where's you hid it! Tell me and I'll let you go! Ooooooh, he's getting mad. Really really mad. I can keep a secret.

ISAAC: Jesus, Jake! Don't be a fucking child! Stop it! I'm not telling! I'm getting mad now! I'm getting mad! Let go of me! It's a secret! That's it, lard ass!

Lights fade to black as they continue wrestling.

JACOB: Lard ass! Bring it on, pipsqueak. Noogie time!

ISAAC: God, it's like trying to grab a walrus! Bag tag!

Black out.

The End.